BATH BUNS AND CHOCOLATE OLIVERS

BATH BUNS AND CHOCOLATE OLIVERS

A Bath Childhood

Rosamund Willoughby

First published in the United Kingdom in 2004 by
The Hobnob Press, PO Box 1838, East Knoyle, Salisbury SP3 6FA

British Library Cataloguing in Publication Data: A catalogue record for this book is available from the British Library.

ISBN 0-946418-26-8

The cover illustrations are by Judy Willoughby. Line drawings in the text are by Ann Hibbs and the Author.

Typeset in 12/16pt Scala. Typesetting and origination by John Chandler
Printed in Great Britain by Salisbury Printing Company Ltd, Salisbury

Contents

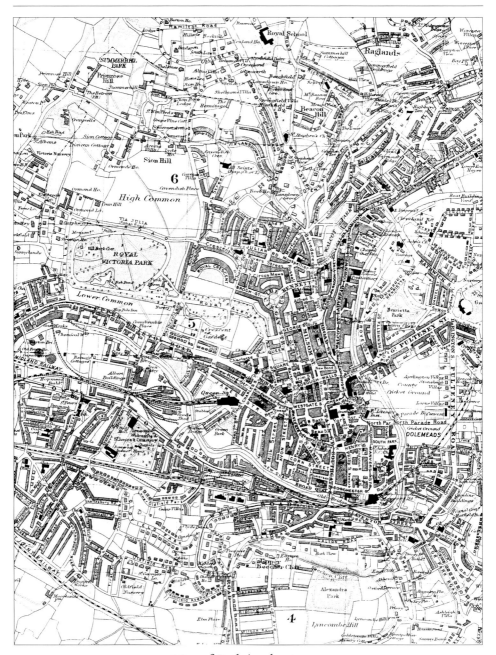

Map of Bath in about 1910

An Introduction

A WHITE RABBIT called 'VEAM' short for 'Victoria Elizabeth Anne Mary' who came from the rather dark and smelly little pet shop in Walcot Street and used to escape and like Peter Rabbit run among the cabbages in the vegetable garden and often reduce me to tears of frustration when trying to catch her, and a pair of green budgerigars called 'Beau' and 'Geste', we were keen followers of Douglas Fairbanks Senior and the current film was Beau Geste; these three were an important part of the lives of Angie and Jean two inseparable friends who grew up together in Bath where their grandparents were living in the early years of the twentieth century.

Today Bath is an 'honey pot' for tourists and visitors from all over the world and traffic lights and one way streets attempt to control the multitude of cars which choke up the entire city as they battle for space in the multi story car parks, but then when we were young a long, long time ago there was plenty of room for everyone, and you could go where you liked and those with cars were able to park anywhere for as long as they needed.

The streets still have their same familiar names but they have changed, Milsom Street lined with beautiful shops was paved with wood blocks which must have made it wonderfully quiet in the days of carriages with their clattering horses, the blocks have disappeared under tarmac, while the crescents and squares and many of the streets were still paved with cobblestones, hard wearing and probably a welcome improvement on mud, today only the sweep of the Royal Crescent and little Queen Street running down through its archway to 'Upper Boro Walls', a small section of the original city walls, still have cobbles. By as early as 1912 when I was born most of the horses had gone from the streets, cars had appeared and there was an excellent network of trams which even climbed to the top of Combe Down though not up the steep Lansdown Hill. Only the baker and milkman and the coal carts were still pulled by horses. We had bicycles and of course everyone walked, the distances are not great and there are plenty of short cuts so it was no hardship.

We bumped on our bikes over the cobbles on our way to and from school, swam in the old swimming baths in the rather smelly steamy water which still came from the hot springs, just as the Romans had done hundreds of years ago, accompanied by the shouts from the Cross Bath nearby which was free for all.

We went to parties and later to dances in the Pump Room, where we would wander down the stairs to the dimly lit and rather romantic Roman baths just as our parents had done before us.

We visited the Assembly Rooms for 'tea dances' or the cinema in the big ballroom, cheapest tickets for the front rows sixpence, with a pianist thumping out sound effects on an upright piano.

We rowed and picnicked and sometimes swam in the river, and had very energetic 'paper chases' up through the labyrinth of small lanes to the top of Lansdown, just imagine the excitement about that in today's litter conscious world, although they were only tiny pieces of paper which blew away dissolving in the rain in no time. The paper,

Five Lansdown Place West

packed into satchels for the 'hares' who led the chase, was chopped up for us in the Pitman's printing works on the Lower Bristol Road, because the children of Ernest and Alfred Pitman, the two sons of Sir Isaac Pitman who invented of shorthand were a part of our gang of friends.

We had a wonderfully happy time with no T.V., mobile phones or computers and this is how it all began.

Well over one hundred years ago my grandmother Scott who was living in India with grandfather, a judge in the Indian Civil Service, decided that if any of her children were to survive she must bring them home to England. So, leaving grandpa in Bombay, she came back to live in Bath with Malcolm the eldest, Roger my father and Mabel the only daughter.

The house she chose was Number Five Lansdown Place West, a tall four storied house halfway down the steep hill at the far end of the beautiful gently curving Lansdown Crescent overlooking the city below.

There the three children grew up, the two boys Malcolm and Roger going to Bath College the boys school at the foot of North Road which has gone through many changes and is now an hotel.

When Roger left school he joined the Gloucestershire Militia, the equivalent of the Territorial Army and later was commissioned into the Gloucestershire Regiment, taking part in the South African war.

Not long after he returned home he met and married my mother Muriel Owen, and they went to live in a small house in Filton close to the regimental depot and here in October 1912 I was born.

The house where grannie Scott settled 'Number Five' as it was always called, was the happy secure background to most of my childhood, the base to which we returned so often.

Very little has changed really, the bumpy cobbles have nearly all gone and so has the attractive curved metal hood over the front door, this probably disappeared during the second world war when in 1942 Bath was bombed and the West Wing suffered badly from fire.

The steeply sloping field opposite the houses with its railings is still there, although there are no longer cows grazing, and the very wide pavement where we bowled our Christmas hoops is just the same.

The last house in the Crescent and the first one of Lansdown Place West used to belong to William Beckford and were connected by a

covered corridor with windows on either side forming an arched entrance to the Mews behind.

Although Beckford had died in his Crescent house in 1844 it was still within living memory of my grandparents generation and he was often talked about. The two houses contained (still do I believe) his furniture and books, together with other reminders of him in and around the area, and so because his name was mentioned and we passed his houses daily, we children imagined that he was still alive and might appear at any time to demand what we were doing trespassing on his private path.

This path with a small iron gate ran up from the Mews behind the Crescent through woods to his tower on the top of Lansdown Hill, it certainly added spice to our secret use of that path.

Beckford's Tower

The tower where he spent a great deal of time working in the library has spectacular views and he surrounded it with an arboretum of rare trees, when he died he chose to be buried up there. The tower and library have recently been restored, although the gardens were taken over some time ago as a cemetery, and both my grandparents are buried there.

Dear much loved Aunt Mabel, about whom more later, is up there as well although she has joined rather unusual company.

When she died aged one hundred and was cremated, my cousin Ruth and I took her ashes up intending to put them with her parents, but in spite of searching for several hours we could find no trace of their grave, although we identified some splendid and unusual trees in what used to be the arboretum!

Instead we decided to put her under a flowering shrub at the centre of a large raised mound which is said to be where Beckford's favourite horse is buried, at least we shall always be able to find her again and I am sure that she would enjoy the joke!

The outside of 'Number Five' as it was known to all and sundry, has hardly changed except for that canopy over the front door, although I am sure that there will have been many changes inside most for the better. For me it will always remain an enchanted time capsule of a long gone age, a happy and welcoming home.

The Houses

ALTHOUGH BOTH SETS of grandparents lived in Bath, their houses were very different, the Scotts, my father's parents lived in Number 5 Lansdown Place West in the west wing of Lansdown Crescent, a tall house sandwiched between numbers four and six, with a long narrow garden at the back.

Lansdown Crescent is the highest of the series of beautiful crescents climbing like giant steps up the steep south facing side of Lansdown Hill. Built during the great building boom of the 18th century, when Ralph Allan the city's Post Master realised that Bath stone was something special, it is a beautiful golden stone easily cut and shaped, perfect for building.

(With great foresight Ralph Allen bought the quarry from which most of the stone came, and of course made his fortune along the way because those were the years of the two great architects the Woods, John

Lansdown Crescent in the background, with Lansdown Place West to the left

senior and junior, together they planned and built the Bath we know today.)

My mother's parents, the Owens home was Richmond House in Weston Park one of a number of substantial family houses surrounded by gardens with their own stables and carriage house, although by now the horses had gone and the carriage house held a car.

Weston Park lies on the outskirts of Bath between the far end of Victoria Park, the 'Common', and the village of Weston, these houses had been individually built and each one was different.

The Scotts had been living in Bath ever since Grannie came back from India in the mid 19th century but the Owen's lived in Devizes before moving to Bath in the early 20th century. The Devizes house is the corner house at the top of Long Street, number 31, with a good sized garden at the back.

Here I am going to digress because this was where I was introduced to buns, not those elegant Bath buns of later years but the delicious down to earth sticky sugary fruity real Wiltshire 'Lardy buns'.

By now, and I was still very young, my eldest uncle was living in number 31, and across the road down Bridewell Street was Barlows the bakers sadly long since gone, a dark little shop with a step down into it and a bell on a spring which tinkled loudly when the door was opened, the bakery was at the back and smelled delicious. I was given one penny and sent to buy the buns, that penny bought me four square hot sticky 'Lardies' at a farthing each, four farthings to a penny you remember!

Richmond House, Weston Park

Number Five

B UT BACK TO THE HOUSES, like most of the Bath houses 'Number Five' had a double cellar, the first one down a flight of stone stairs from the hall held the big kitchen and other interesting places like the maids sitting room, and below that again was the coal cellar a dark and spooky place which I was never brave enough to explore!

Above these were three floors each with two large rooms and one or more smaller ones like grandpa's 'snug' or a bathroom, and the attics

bathrooms, they must have got through a lot of coal, but it was very cheap indeed in those days.

Nearly all deliveries were done by horse drawn vans and when the drivers stopped for a rest or their lunch or whatever, they would hang a hessian bag of oats over the horses neck for him to dip his nose into, hence the term 'nose bag' which we still use today.

At the very bottom of Lansdown Hill on the left hand side was the Vets surgery with a cobbled yard, he probably dealt more with horses in those days than cats or dogs. Outside on the road side wall was a large notice intended as a warning to hauliers to consider their horses when pulling heavy loads up Bath's steep hills. Made of blue enamel with two pictures of horses heads side by side, one had its head held firmly down by the reins, the other was loose with its head up and free, the notice read 'Not like this' under the head down but 'like this' under the head up and free. A horse would have needed to be able to put its head up when straining to pull uphill, the notice remained there for many years after the vet and horses had gone. I wonder what happened to it?

Even more exciting and eagerly awaited were the occasional visits of the barrel organ man, he would push his heavy organ up the hill and stop in the road outside, you could tell he was on his way because the music gradually came closer as he worked his way round the streets.

'Our' barrel organ man did not have a monkey but his loud cheerful tinkling music as he turned the handle playing all the popular songs of the moment, I thought was wonderful, family and neighbours were not so enthusiastic and after being sent out to put some money into his old top hat he would be firmly told to move on!

Outside the dining room, stone uncarpeted stairs led down to the basement kitchen and up and down those stairs some poor little maid or perhaps she was elderly I do not remember, had to carry large trays laden with heavy dishes and plates to the dining room. There was what was called a butlers tray outside the door, a large mahogany tray with deep sides which rested on a folding stand, a sort of halfway house for loading and unloading.

Five Lansdown Place West

All kinds of interesting things happened down these stairs, it really was 'below stairs'. There was the large kitchen whose only windows were high up on one side because of course the room was below ground level so it always had the light on by day or night. At the far end stood the big 'range' a carefully black leaded monster fired by coal, which had to be cleaned out and re-lit very early every morning, a dirty and sometimes tricky job, because they were all temperamental and hard to manage according to the wind.

Ranges had a large flat top with several circular lids which lifted off to the fire below for kettles and saucepans, and several ovens all controlled by a series of 'dampers' which could be opened and shut to make or stop the draught, plus a water tank for hot water at one side, with a small brass tap at the front; this together with a good many brass knobs and a large flat brass fender were all kept highly polished.

Down a flight of steps from the pavement was a small open space known as the 'area' here was the tradesmen's entrance never called the back door! This opened on to a wide stone paved passageway where stood the knife sharpener, a contraption which consisted of a large rough stone wheel turned by a big iron handle, no stainless steel in those days and this kept the knives highly polished and lethally sharp, but it also tended to wear them out.

Somewhere off this passageway was the maids sitting room, a very cosy and special place into which I was occasionally invited as a treat for tea. I do not think it was very big, with a window looking out into the area and an open fireplace with hobs on either side and a highly polished copper kettle singing away. There were comfortable looking

Outside Number Five. Grandpa Scott with baby Angie (1912) and Roger her father

wicker armchairs with cushions and lots of china ornaments on the mantelpiece with a substantial tea laid on the central table. I have no idea how many maids grannie kept but there certainly would have been a cook, parlour maid and housemaid with a young scullery or kitchen maid and what was called a charlady to do the rough scrubbing of all those stone floors once a week. In the mornings the maids wore washable print dresses, Grannie's were pink, with big white aprons, like a nurses apron and a white cap, after lunch they would go up all those ninety stairs to wash and change into tidy black serge dresses with little frilly muslin aprons and caps to match, ready to answer the door to visitors.

Social life followed an ordered and well understood pattern much of which continued until the second world war. 'Calling' with 'visiting cards' was a minefield of complicated etiquette in itself, who left cards and when and which had the corners turned down and why!

In Grannie's day any hostess who knew her business had a regular day on which it was understood that she would be 'at home' to visitors, Grannie's was a Thursday when a special dainty tea would be served in the formal drawing room upstairs, on the whole they were friendly happy occasions.

A day was set aside each week for baking and although there was often a delicious looking cake on the dining room table it was strictly not for cutting, no, we were told that is for Thursday. It remained a family joke for many years after 'at home' days were long forgotten for someone to see an uncut cake on the tea table and to ask 'may we cut the cake or is it for Thursday?'

The wide staircase winding its way up from the ground floor to the attics was of wood and well carpeted with little half landings between each floor. On the first of these there was a bamboo table covered with a fascinating cloth embroidered all over with dozens of tiny circular glass mirrors, brought back from India I expect.

Drawing rooms were usually upstairs on the first floor, the one at 'Number Five' was above the entrance hall and dining room the whole width of the house. A long wide high ceilinged room with three large sash windows facing south over the street and view beyond, with a fireplace at the far end, a beautiful room.

Jane Scott née Hungerford (Grannie)

The doorway leading in from the landing was very deeply recessed with a heavy curtain against the draught, making it a good place to hide when the curtain was drawn.

This was very much Grannie's room and was filled with her treasures from the Indian days all of which were fascinating to a child. In front of the fire was an enormous tiger skin rug, the tiger must have been shot by Grandpa because you certainly would not buy one shot by some-one else, it really must have been very large because I can remember sitting on the head and sliding down its neck, it is extraordinary but I can still feel that soft silky fur today. There was a large round brass tray on folding ebony legs with twenty brass elephants, they were all slightly different and had probably been collected over several years, marching round it heads to tails, the largest about fourteen inches high down to a tiny one of only an inch and a half the table has vanished over the years but those elephants are still very much alive!

As in most drawing rooms even today there were several small tables with all sorts of ornaments, pieces of china and silver but best of all were the bangles of every description threaded on to special rods, there were silver and gold ones, glass of every colour under the sun, jewelled ones, fat ones and thin ones all beautiful, and when grandpa died and grannie and Aunt Mabel moved down to a ground floor flat at the top of Park Street, all these treasures moved with them.

On the same floor as the drawing room were two other rooms, grandpa and grannies bedroom and 'the cat gallery', this was their 'loo' and was so called because every inch of the walls and the back of the door were covered with pictures of cats, there were postcards and old calendars and pictures cut out of magazines, comic and colourful, all the family and friends knew about the 'cat gallery' and would add to the collection from time to time, it was an absolutely fascinating place to sit. The loo itself was rather special although not at all unusual in those days, there was a wide polished mahogany shelf stretching from wall to wall with a hinged section in the centre which lifted up to reveal the seat. To one side was a rather splendid china handle labelled 'pull' let into a recess in the shelf which operated a plunger to flush the loo.

On the next floor up there were two more bedrooms, Aunt Mabel's and the one where we slept and grandpa's 'snug'. The thing I remember best is the bath in front of the fire, there would be a beautiful hot fire burning in the grate and in front of it on a big bath mat the 'hip bath', an enamelled metal bath white inside and painted a mustardy yellow outside with a raised back. I suppose they were called hip baths because a grown up could only sit up in it and lean against the back rather like an armchair, but a child could get right down into the hot water.

No-one who has not experienced the delight of sitting in a hot bath in front of a blazing fire can have any idea of how lovely it was, and there cannot be many today who have, and then the final pleasure of being wrapped in a large fluffy white bath towel beautifully warmed in front of the fire.

This only happened at Number Five the other grandparents had a proper bathroom - although that was quite special too.

In case you are thinking of some poor person carrying all that hot water up all those stairs do not worry, there was a bathroom next to Aunt Mabel's bedroom where the water was heated by a gas fired geyser. Geysers in those days were rather temperamental and alarming, tall copper cylinders, they were noisy and could explode if wrongly handled but they must have been very welcome when they were first invented.

Aunt Mabel's bedroom faced over the garden at the back and had a most interesting fire place, for a child anyway, the large mantelpiece was covered with green felt or baize with a deep scalloped frill ending in dozens of small plush bobbles, into which she had pinned every paper flag from the many 'flag days' in aid of various good causes, a colourful array and endlessly fascinating to a little girl.

Flag days also had a different spin-off when I thought that it seemed a very simple way of adding to my meagre pocket money. I made myself a small tray from a shoe box lid and hung it from a tape round my neck filled it with some of the collection of flags and went and stood on the busy street corner nearby, until an uncle appeared and was very angry, hauling me off home with a severe lecture. I have never forgotten it but now I think that he lacked a sense of humour and could have handled it better!

Grandpa and Grannie Scott who were known as Pater and Mater, were a charming knowledgeable pair full of laughter and fun.

Grannie was the youngest of a family of girls whose mother had died, there were six of them brought up by their father by the sea in County Cork in Ireland, and judging by tales they told me as a child and cuttings from local newspapers they were an extremely lively lot!

Grannie was Jane but always known as Janie, with beautiful deep chestnut red hair, they were a family of redheads Aunt Mabel's being real brilliant carroty red and my father like his mother chestnut red. She must have worn colours at some time but I only remember her in black, with high necks and little white pleated frills, her dresses remained ankle length all her life regardless of fashion.

I remember two of the aunts, Mina, Wilhelmina, the eldest and Gussie, Augusta and those two I loved dearly.

Grandpa Scott was a delightful and loving man, bearded as were so many in those days (I was born in 1912). A keen botanist he was instrumental in the planning of Bath's Botanical Gardens in Victoria Park. We spent many happy hours strolling hand in hand around the local roads and lanes and although I did not appreciate it at the time, I know now how much he taught me, not only the names of the trees and flowers but how to use my eyes. The names of the wild flowers in the fields and hedgerows or growing in the walls were common knowledge to me, constantly repeated and even now when I see an ivy leaved toadflax I find myself saying the name and am carried back to a small ledge in a wall on one of the steepest parts of Lansdown Hill just below St. Stephen's Church!

Grandpa was also a keen gardener although the garden was only a long fairly narrow strip, the width of the house, I suppose, down to a high wall at the end where a door opened out on to a wide grass area common to all the houses. Here I had my very first garden, a tiny patch by the side of the path just in front of the water butt, I can only remember the pansies.

Like most of his generation he was a great collector, everyone had albums and scrapbooks often beautifully hand decorated and painted, those which have survived are increasingly valuable and precious but far too many were just thrown

Matthew Scott 'Pater' (Grandpa)

away. He collected crests, most peoples notepaper had an embossed family crest as did the flap on the envelopes; and albums of postcards, and newspaper cuttings galore. All these were kept in what was known as his 'snug' a long narrow room with a window at the far end, next door to the night nursery, high up and looking down over Bath, several large tables all piled high with books and papers, the walls lined with bookshelves.

He would wait in the evenings until I was tucked up in bed, my bed was next to the door, and the light was out and my mother had gone downstairs, and then come and sit on the bed and tell me stories. It was always the same one which continued night after night whenever we were staying there, all about a make believe family called the 'wobbly jim jocks'. I have no idea now what it was about other than the name but we enjoyed ourselves until he was summoned downstairs for dinner.

Perhaps I didn't always go to sleep straight away it must have been rather quiet and lonely when everyone else was shut away down several flights of stairs, anyway once when I was very small I came down in my nightie from our bedroom, collected the elderly cat, no easy task as it was large and heavy, and together we crept into my grandparents big bed, right down to the bottom where we slept happily in a safe warm cavern.

Grandpa Scott outside Number Five with Angie aged 18 months, 1914

There must have been some anxious searching and calling all over the house, I have often wondered how we were found, did they notice the bump in the bed or perhaps the cat emerged when hearing the voices calling?

Richmond House

RICHMOND HOUSE WAS BUILT long after the great 18th century building boom and was very different from 'Number 5', a long low two storied house with a wide verandah running the whole length of the front.

No basement kitchen here instead a spacious light and airy room with three windows on to the verandah facing the small front garden. There was still a big coal fired range but things had moved on by then, and

Richmond House

David Owen, Angie's Grandpa

there was now a gas cooker as well. Although the drawing room and dining room had open grates with coal fires, all the bedrooms and the nurseries on the top floor were heated by gas fires.

On the south side of the house was the dining room with a glass conservatory leading out of it , always filled with colourful plants, this was Grandpa's domain, Grannie had her writing desk at the far end so it was quite companionable and unless the weather was really cold the doors into the conservatory were kept open and Grandpa could escape out into the garden that way.

At the fireplace end he had a comfortable red leather armchair with his box of cigars and their paraphernalia on a small table by his right-hand, and on the left in a deep recess the very latest in gramophones with a really wonderful collection of records.

He was a great card player and would sit up at the dining table in his big 'carver' chair, this meant that his back was to the fire so to shield him from the heat a specially made shield hooked on to the chair back, it was made of basketwork covered in red baize which stretched from above his head right down to the floor.

Clockwork toys were all the rage and Grandpa was a keen collector; the table would be cleared to show off the latest acquisition, the variety was astonishing from somersaulting circus clowns to a motor bike and side car with driver and passenger which circled the table and could go into reverse, he loved them all and so did we.

The room next door was the drawing room not upstairs but on the ground floor, this was Grannie's favourite room with a wide bow window and glass doors leading out on to a sunny terrace. No tiger skin or bangles instead, because Grannie and her family were musical there was a lovely grand piano, and we all spent many happy hours standing round her singing together.

This Grannie had given up 'at home' days instead she had tea parties where she presided over the tea making ceremony. There would be a silver tray with tea pot, milk jug and sugar bowl, and a silver caddy containing the tea with a caddy spoon and most important, the silver kettle on its stand over a little menthylated spirit heater. I think that the water was probably about boiling when it came in, the little heater would surely have taken rather a long time.

The cakes, bread and butter and tiny sandwiches were carried round on a three tiered cake stand with a handle over the top, it was just as formal as with Grannie Scott using the prettiest china tea set. On ordinary days tea was on the dining room table and much less formal, but no dripping teas!

Lilian Owen née Peake (Grannie)

Upstairs on the first floor were the main bedrooms leading off a long passage with a loo at each end, no interesting cat gallery here. A large bathroom with a fireplace though I do not think it was ever lit, the bath itself was a splendid one large and deep, panelled in polished mahogany with a wide mahogany shelf all round the top, it was directly above the kitchen. This caused trouble with the cook because there often seemed to be more than one of us in the bath at the same time and the noise and splashing became more like a flood on the floor which tended to seep through the kitchen ceiling, bringing a furious cook upstairs, it was wise to keep the door locked.

Two staircases led up from the landing one at each end, the first to the nurseries and the other at the far end to the maid's bedrooms, below this one there was a small 'housemaids pantry' as it was called, where she kept all her cleaning things, with a floor level lead-lined sink with two taps.

The day and night nurseries on the top floor were big spacious rooms with sunny bay windows facing south over the garden, heated by gas fires with the usual high mesh nursery fireguards.

The day nursery held all sorts of treasures, a beautiful dolls house, which stood on the floor, handsome in red brick (painted of course) with a little panelled mahogany front door complete with brass handle and door knocker, this had been especially made for my mother and her two sisters, Lillian and

Granny Owen with baby Angie. The photograph is inscribed 'Just short coated'

Marjorie, by the Devizes local carpenter for their nursery at number 31 Long Street, in their childhood. I still have it, now well over 100 years old.

Several boxes of wooden bricks, one of polished oak, another of large building blocks of various sizes and one very attractive 'Sussex Village', a complete model village made out of wood, each building beautifully coloured, church, farm house and buildings, manor house lots of cottages and a school, I still have some of the bricks but sadly the Sussex Village has vanished.

There was a beautiful little cane backed and seated mahogany chair which could be used with a matching small table, or the chair could stand on top of the table with a wooden bolt to hold it firmly together which made it into a high chair with a small bar across the front to prevent the baby from falling out, that too I still possess and use for dolls tea parties for great grandchildren.

The largest and most interesting piece of furniture was a heavy four fold screen, the sides were covered all over with a fascinating assortment of pictures, these were advertisements and pictures cut out of old magazines or calendars, animals, flowers, characters from books, events like royal weddings or coronations, with any gaps filled in with hand drawn and painted pictures some by quite well known artists; all painted over with clear varnish, a real treasure, who had made it or where it ended up I will never know which is sad. The adjoining room which later became my bedroom was the night nursery.

Unlike 'Number 5' which had a long narrow garden at the back with high walls on either side, Richmond House on the corner of Weston Road and Weston Park was surrounded by a mature garden, with beautiful trees.

An old mulberry tree, many Bath gardens have mulberry trees there must have been a fashion for them at some time, ours was on the upper lawn giving shade to summer teas outside, and to those watching the players on the lower croquet lawn. There was a hornbeam tree and a very tall spreading flowering cherry, with a swing which because it hung from a rather high branch had an exceptionally long swinging range.

Grandpa loved his garden especially the fruit, he did not actually work in the garden himself, there was an elderly gardener called Beer, but he was very knowledgeable. Down at the stable end was the vegetable garden hidden away behind a tall yew hedge, this is where the white rabbit 'Veam' lived and escaped, with a medlar tree whose twisted branches were splendid for climbing, medlars have peculiar brown fruit which are not ready for eating until they are almost rotten, a very acquired taste, Grandpa loved them!

Peach trees grew against the south wall facing the croquet lawn with a garden seat in front of them, I can still see Grandpa sitting in the sun eating a freshly picked ripe peach!

His other favourite was violets, grown especially for Grannie in one of a row of glass topped frames, deep purple long stemmed and with a

The Garden at Richmond House

delicious scent, I had my small strip of garden between two apple trees close to these violet frames.

Much further down on one side of the vegetable garden close to the stables and well hidden from the house we were given a Wendy House. A small wooden one room house with a large window and a front door complete with brass door knocker in the shape of a New Forest pony, set in its own small garden and surrounded by a low picket fence with a gate to the path leading up to the front door.

A kind and thoughtful uncle found and installed on paving stones a small army surplus cast iron stove with a tall chimney in a fenced off section of the garden, where we could boil a kettle and fry sausages to our hearts content in perfect safety.

The house itself was furnished with a bench seat and several shelves, a table and two stools and a child's folding chair which for some reason became known as 'me only', I am not sure why or which of us was the 'me', but 'me only' continued to be known by that name long after my childhood!

Various people gave us things to help furnish, my mother produced a large blue enamel teapot, and there were curtains and some cushions, a table cloth and a kettle, saucepan and frying pan, probably discards from the house, the rest was up to us.

Woolworths right down at the bottom of the town was where we did most of our shopping. In those days it really was the 'sixpenny and three penny store', nothing was sold over sixpence, although they could get round that by charging separately for things like a cup and saucer. They sold absolutely everything even garden seeds, and bit by bit we collected our china, blue and white stripes, knives and forks and kitchen spoons, etc., it took a long time because our pocket money of sixpence a week was needed for other necessities like sweets as well.

There were two candle lamps and an enamel washing up bowl, the water came from the stable tap. We spent hours and hours busy and happy in and around the Wendy House and often had visitors, and on the last day of every holiday we had supper down there.

There would be Jean, Honor, Ruth and myself and the 'menu' never varied, Campbell's vegetable soup provided by Jean's mother, baked beans, sausages and tins of fruit salad.

The 'Wendy House', early days. Left to Right: Jean, Ruth, Angie

As we walked down through the town on our visits to Woolworths we would sometimes pause and watch the people who visited the very old fountain to have a drink of the Bath water from a constantly flowing tap.

Goodness knows how many years that fountain must have stood there it was very old, a substantial ornate affair of carved Bath stone standing on a small island at the entrance to the

Colonnade just opposite the doors to the Roman Baths. There was a lead pipe from which the hot, steamy and smelly water flowed non-stop directly from the old springs below, into a stone trough. to one side was a very battered small lead cup fastened to the wall by a chain and all sorts of people stopped to drink their daily dose of what I suppose they believed were Bath's healing waters. A few rinsed the cup before dropping it clanking down on its chain for the next person! There were many others presumably in Bath for 'the cure' who brought their thermos flasks to fill and take home. We never drank the water ourselves but found it fascinating to watch.

Drinking at the Fountain

'Grafton'

A FTER SPENDING SOME TIME living in 'rooms' we eventually moved into a home of our own, 'Grafton', a small semi-detached house at the top of Park Lane, on the corner of Weston Road, only a very short distance from the grandparents at Richmond House.

'Grafton' had belonged to a very old lady some relation of my Grandfather Scott, a Miss Alice Howell-Walsh. I was once taken to visit her as a very small child and all I can remember is that she gave me a pretty little silver teaspoon with a filigree handle which I have to this day.

When we first lived there an old blind man appeared every day, I think some one brought him, he had an umbrella for wet days and some shelter from over hanging trees. He would sit up against the wall outside our gate on a box or camp stool and sell matches from a little tray, old people selling matches was quite a common sight. He cannot have made much but it probably gave him a little more dignity than begging.

The opposite side of the road was all open fields with cows most of the year and all the pleasure and fun of wild flowers and hay making in the summer. The field is now a part of Victoria Park with an imposing pillared entrance in place of the old five barred wooden farm gate.

Right at the top of the house in the attic, next door to Alice the maid's bedroom there was the nursery, a long room with a sloping ceiling on one side which came right down to the floor and a single window.

This window looked across to the house next door directly into a large studio, which was a constant source of interest to us, but for Mr. Lawrence the head of Bath School of Art whose studio this was, we must have been a distracting nuisance. The window was barred because the drop below was the height of the house on to a paved path up to the front door. However quite oblivious of the danger and totally confidant in the screws which held the bars we managed to thread ourselves through them to hang out over the abyss, and that was the only time that Mr. Lawrence reacted and react he did in no uncertain fashion, flinging open his own large window he bellowed at us to 'get inside at once'!

The nursery held several treasures some of which sadly have been thrown away when replaced by a newer model or when moving house.

There was the beautiful doll's house which had been made for my mother and her two sisters by the local carpenter in Devizes, now well over 100 years old, which has been played with by countless little girls and which still has several of the original pieces of furniture, including an upright piano complete with tiny candles and a hall stand with pegs, a mirror and place for umbrellas, both made of painted tin.

A wonderful dolls tea and dinner set in white enamel decorated with little pink rosebuds, dozens of pieces, slightly chipped but otherwise

complete and now nearly ninety years old which continue to give many happy dolls parties.

Probably the best of all was my own father's gramophone given to me by my Grandmother, one of the very early models, exactly like the 'His masters Voice' trade mark. A square wooden box with the turntable on top and a handle on one side with which to wind it up, one wind usually managed a complete record! And a large megaphone shaped loudspeaker, we only needed a small dog to complete the picture.

With it came a lovely stack of old '78' records, which we played so often that I think we knew everyone by heart, there were all the popular music hall songs and sentimental ballads, several Harry Lauder including 'The Laughing Policeman', and what we were allowed in those far off days to call 'Negro Spirituals' without causing anyone any offence!

The house was lit by gas, and gas lighting required matches, but many of the lights, in the hall or the centre of a room were too high to reach, instead there was a simple arrangement called a 'by-pass', a tiny jet of flame permanently alight, nearby there would be a pole with a hook on the end to pull down a little chain which turned on the gas which lit with a loud pop, the same thing happened to turn it off again.

Although Grafton had a proper bathroom with

a basin, there were no basins in the bedrooms instead there were marble topped washstands.

The washstands were elaborately equipped, there would be two basins with jugs of cold water, one large and one small, and an amazing assortment of dishes of all shapes and sizes for tooth brushes etc., and a soap dish with a lid. Below the basins would be a 'slop pail' (a china bucket with a lid) and probably a deep oval footbath (much sought after today by flower arrangers!) and of course a chamber pot, two if it was a double room, all made of decorated china, with wreaths of rosebuds or flowers of some sort.

A maid would bring brass cans of hot water and cover them with a giant padded 'tea cosy' to keep them hot.

Some bedrooms had gas fires but they were only lit when we were ill or perhaps dressing for a party, so with no electric blankets the beds could be very cold indeed in winter. We did have hot water bottles if we were lucky which helped, there were several kinds of hot water bottles, the most usual were the 'stone' ones, a large Swiss roll shape with a flat base and a hole with a screw stopper for filling it with hot water, made of heavy china these held the heat well but were not at all cuddly. Mine was made of copper, round and rather like a squat kettle without a spout or handle, it was painfully hot to touch unless wrapped in a woolly vest!

When we had coughs and colds most families had simple remedies passed down from mother to daughter which were easily made up at home. My mother kept the necessary ingredients for her mixture in small glass bottles inside a polished mahogany medicine chest with a brass handle and a key.

I have the recipe still:

½ teaspoon Paregoric
1 teaspoon Ipecacuanha wine
1 teaspoon sweet spirit of Nitre
1 teaspoon Syrop of Squills
1 very large tablespoon of golden syrup.
Mix all the ingredients together with 1 pint boiling water and allow to cool.
Take one large medicine glass full three times a day.

It tasted horrible and we were allowed one or two of the tiny little Frys chocolate creams. I cannot remember whether it did us any good!

Camphorated oil rubbed into the chest at bedtime completed the cure!

Downstairs in the sunny little kitchen Alice as well as the cooking and housework dealt with the ironing. The sheets and towels all 'went out' to one of the many women who 'took in laundry', so it was only small household things, blouses, dresses and handkerchiefs, etc.

She used the kitchen table with several thicknesses of blanket covered with a sheet and 'flat irons', no ironing boards or electric irons in those days.

In the grandparents houses which still had coal fired ranges, the irons stood on end in front of the open fire to heat them, but Alice had a gas cooker and her irons were heated on top. There were always several irons because as one cooled it would be exchanged for a hot one, they were solid and held the heat well and needed a padded holder, the recognised way to test for the right heat was to spit on it, a good quick sizzle and it was ready!

Sundays and the Churches

S UNDAY WAS CHURCH DAY, and nothing much happened until after the eleven o' clock service. The services were always the same every Sunday, Communion at eight o' clock, Matins at eleven and Evensong at six, so there was no excuse for forgetting the times, and the churches were full.

The church that we attended depended on which of the grandparents we were with at the time. From Richmond House it was 'St. Andrews', a large city church on an island surrounded by roads, at the St. James's Square end of Julian Road. From 'Number Five' it would be little 'All Saints' below the West Wing of the Crescent.

Sadly neither church exists today, St. Andrews had a direct hit and was destroyed in the 1942 bombing raids, all that remains today is a levelled ruin in a grassed area with a memorial stone recording its history.

While All Saints which also suffered bomb damage is no longer a church having been converted into a dwelling house, which I suppose is better than being bombed out of existence.

All Saints was Grandpa and Grannie Scott's church, below the end of Lansdown Crescent immediately above Park Street. We would walk down the small curved lane with chestnut trees on the left hand side and a steep grassy bank golden in the spring with celandine. Grandpa and I took our time strolling down hand in hand there was much to see and discuss, those must have been the first wild flowers whose name I learned and even today I watch eagerly every spring for the first celandine to open and am transported back over the years.

As far as I can remember the outside of the church was not very impressive, while the inside was circular, low and rather dark. In those days it was quite usual for regular members of the congregation to have their own allotted pew or place in a pew marked by a small metal frame screwed on to the prayer book shelf into which a visiting card could be slotted, lesser folk or less regular visitors sat at the back!

I think that All Saints was quite a well off little church with the congregation coming largely from the big houses in the nearby Crescents. The Rector, a Mr. Powell, a short little man with a mass of snow white hair lived with his family in one of the largest houses at the centre of the Crescent.

St. Andrews church was a typical large town church and for some reason was the one chosen by Grandpa and Grannie Owen rather than the nearer one in Weston village. We would all pack into Grandpa's large chauffeur driven Armstrong Sidley to be driven the mile or so to church and afterwards we younger ones used up our energy by walking home.

My mother and I sat with the grandparents up in the front immediately below the pulpit. While friends, aunts, uncles and cousins were dotted about in other parts of the church, and we children would remain standing up as the rest of the congregation sat down so that we could spot each other before being pulled down by angry parents.

It is strange to think that the church which was so much a part of our childhood is nothing more than a heap of stones today with hardly anyone left to remember the time when it was filled with music and singing.

The War Years

BEFORE WE GO ANY FURTHER I must return to the year 1912 the year when I was born, and how long ago that seems today, only just into the twentieth century, so many changes and two world wars which finished forever a way of life which had continued unaltered for centuries.

Not long before my second birthday Germany overran neutral little Belgium and the 1914-18 war began. The Gloucestershire regiment was sent to France as part of the expeditionary force, they seem to have had very short notice and my father only had time for a short letter home to his mother:

London January 1st 1915

My Dearest Mummie,

I am off to the front tomorrow morning, a wire came this afternoon saying that I had to leave at once to join the expeditionary force . . . I am going down first thing tomorrow morning to Southampton . . . well I am very glad I managed to get down for Christmas, it was very lucky . . . Well, Mummie darling goodbye and God bless you and keep an eye on Angie and Muriel for me if anything happens.

Love to Pater and Mabel

Ever your loving son

Roger

Sadly this was his last Christmas, he died of wounds in October.

My mother took me home to stay with her parents who at that time had moved to Combe Down in Bath. Shortly before my third birthday, in

Roger Scott, Angie's father, killed in World War One at the battle of Loos

1915, my father came home from the horrors of the trenches in France for two weeks leave. He arrived late in the evening after I was asleep, but every minute was precious so I was woken, wrapped in a big white shawl, and carried downstairs to stand barefooted on the dining room table.

I remember to this day the feel of that cold shiny table under my feet before being carried back to bed.

The short time together as a family must have been a happy one, they went shopping for a birthday present and bought my first large toy, a very early model motor car made of plywood and painted green, pedal driven with a seat, steering wheel, bonnet and four wheels. Like most small children I was pretty slow to get the hang of it and was better at going backwards than forwards, much to my father's amusement. That little car lasted for a great many years and after some pretty rough treatment by me and my cousins eventually just fell to pieces.

Those two weeks were all too quickly over and he returned to France and the horrors of that ghastly war, in less than two weeks he was badly wounded in the battle of Loos and died two days later. My poor young mother received the dreaded yellow telegram which was to completely change our lives:-

> Deeply regret to inform you that Captain R D Scott Gloucestershire Regiment died of wounds on October 18th. Lord Kitchener expresses his sorrow.

I suppose my mother felt she could not face Bath with its happy memories and kind and sympathetic friends, anyway we packed up and travelled down to Devon to Torquay where a kind elderly widow the mother of two of her friends gave us a home.

The rest of the war years were spent in Devon, only returning to Bath each Christmas.

Perhaps one of the reasons that we went down to live in Devon was because my mother's eldest sister Lilian was living in the village of Buckfastleigh not far away, with her husband Sam Marle and small daughter Ruth.

We may even have gone there first, I was only three, Ruth two years old and there was baby, John.

It was a busy and cheerful household and my early memories are a rather mixed collection.

Uncle Sam, a very special person, was the local doctor and his practise included Buckfast Abbey with its monks, a much quieter place in those days before it became a tourist attraction. My mother and her sister Lilian were very close as were Ruth and I, she was only eleven months younger, and I virtually grew up in that family, there were two more sisters Elisabeth and Marian later on.

The nursery was a sunny room off the bedroom landing with a window and a deep window seat looking out over the vegetable garden and up to the woods at the top of the hill behind.

The house must have been part of a farm because there was a yard next door and cows came and went. A lane ran up past the side of the house from the road to the woods and was a favourite walk, safe from traffic and not too far. I remember one walk in particular perfectly clearly to this day.

We had reached the top of the lane and the woods and I had probably led Ruth further in among the trees than usual, they were beautiful old 'wind in the willows' type woods, we were called 'time to go home now', we stayed hidden and quiet until finally came 'we are not waiting any longer, we are going home now'.

To be by ourselves with no grown ups seemed exciting and fun until the sound of their voices gradually disappeared in the distance. Then suddenly there were noises in the wood and a vision of Red Riding Hood's wolf seemed very real and we took to our heels and ran and ran back down the lane to safety, we must have been really frightened because it is still real to me today!

The nursery with its linoleum floor, and cheerful fire surrounded by a tall fireguard with a polished brass top, an armchair on one side and a low nursing chair on the other, a big dolls house, a rocking horse and boxes of wooden bricks, was the centre of our little world.

In one corner there was a big table covered in what was called American Cloth or Oil Cloth, with a Windsor chair at one end and a wooden bench down each side, here we sat to eat our meals. The only one I really remember is supper when we had milk jelly and someone read us a story. Milk jellies are made with Chivers jelly cubes melted in hot water and topped up with cold milk, in different fruit flavours and colours they are delicious, poured into a mould to set, ours was a copper mould which when turned out had little turrets all round the top, it was very important to have a turret with ones helping of jelly.

Another treat for supper or if we were not well was 'bread and milk' does anyone make bread and milk today I wonder, it is delicious, a thick slice of white bread is cut into small cubes and put into a cereal bowl with plenty of boiling milk poured over it and lots of crunchy brown sugar, a very comforting thing to eat. Do you remember Mrs Rabbit in Beatrix Potter's 'Peter Rabbit', Flopsy, Mopsy and Cottontail had 'bread and milk with blackberries for supper'?

In Torquay I was introduced to the 'primus', from which my mother was never parted, that little stove sitting on a battered circular tin tray travelled with us wherever we went.

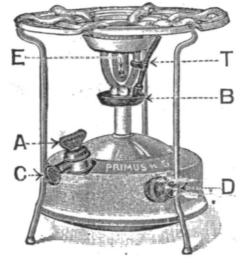

I have happy memories of the primus that noisy rather scary affair requiring constant pumping up to keep it going was a very important part of our lives.

My mother's generation were great sweet makers especially treacle toffee or fudge, an occupation we children entered into with great enthusiasm. How delicious were those illicit teaspoons of the creamy sweet condensed milk made by Nestlés, the basis of all good fudge and that is something which has not changed.

The toffee was a wet day treat a very sticky business, dark golden brown very hard and long lasting.

And then there was the annual January ritual of making marmalade. Early in the month the Seville oranges appeared in the shops, as they still do today, and out would come the big copper preserving pan, this would balance precariously on top of the Primus bubbling away with the marmalade. That well polished copper pan now lives on the dresser shelf in my present day kitchen.

For me the Torquay years were carefree and happy, the war passed over my head, most of our days were spent on the beach at Corbyns Head and it was always summer!

Although I had a very unglamorous baggy bathing dress I couldn't swim, I was a coward and hated the cold water, so we went to the heated sea water swimming pool on the far side of the harbour where I was suspended in a kind of harness from a long pole.

The instructor walked up and down the side of the pool while I struggled in the water, I was scared stiff and made no progress until a visiting uncle, my mother's brother Jack, home on leave, carried me to the deep end and just dropped me in, I sank and can still remember the water closing over my head, like a puppy the instinct for survival took over and I paddled desperately for the side but it worked and I could swim.

In those days Torquay had a wonderful toy shop and as a reward Uncle Jack gave me a very beautiful Swiss musical box which played six different tunes. It wound up with a large key and could be controlled by several levers, it gave us immense pleasure and fun for many years and today is a joy to my own great grandchildren.

Everyone walked in those days. If you wanted to get anywhere you walked and we did our fair share, and how much more there was to see and discover, wild flowers as they came out, birds nests, different coloured empty snail shells and discarded birds eggshells, and in the early spring those delicious peppery little green shoots on the hawthorn or may trees which country children still pick and eat and call 'bread and cheese'.

The country roads and lanes were rough and untarmaced, dusty in summer and muddy in winter, but well cared for, each one with its own road man. There would be heaps of stones dumped at intervals on the roadside for the road man to break up and use to fill in the potholes and these had to be inspected as we passed in case one day a fossil would turn up among them, a real treasure.

Those road men really loved their stretches of road and knew every bird and its nest, where there were frogs and toads or grass snakes taking great care not to disturb them, none of today's wholesale trashing with vicious machines.

A month after my sixth birthday came Armistice Day, November 11th 1918, the war was over at last, and it was time for me to start school.

School

S IX YEARS OLD and now it was time to go to school. So clutching a brand new pencil box in a brand new shoe bag hand in hand with my mother I walked down to the school front door, where a strange woman smiled and handed me on into a noisy chattering mêlée of girls, one of whom led me down a stone staircase into the basement cloakroom, dimly lit with a stone flagged floor and rows of wooden benches with hooks above them for our coats and shoe bags. The rather damp and dark lavatories were down here as well, although I was not brave enough to use them by myself for quite a long time, instead there was a bathroom somewhere near the top of the house. Apart from removing the household furniture little had been done to change a family house into a school.

When I came up the stairs again my mother had vanished, I was lost and frightened as we little ones were hustled up endless stairs to the attic classrooms. I was anxious all the morning until at lunch time when I emerged from the dungeon cloakroom and there, oh joy, was my mother waiting at the door.

The Hermitage House School at the top right hand side of Burlington Street was for girls from six years old right up to leaving age at eighteen. Nearly all of us were day girls although there were a few boarders who lived in another house across the road, both were owned and run by two sisters, the Miss Websters and a little further up the road on the left hand side was a small preparatory school for boys run by their brother Mr. Webster and his wife.

I was soon joined by my younger cousins, Ruth to the girls and little John to Mr. Webster and his boys. These cousins whose father, my uncle, the doctor, now lived in Newbridge Road in Bath and had quite a long walk to and from school each day, so I who was the lucky owner of a bicycle would wait at the top of Park Lane and then all three of us would mount my bike. I stood and pedalled Ruth sat on the saddle and clasped me tightly round the waist, while poor little John sat on the back carrier which would gradually push down on to the wheel with his weight and become very hot indeed, we ignored his cries for help until he became desperate when we made a brief stop for things to cool off. John moved on quite soon to a larger school and Ruth acquired her own bicycle but we continued to join up a the top of Park Lane.

Although we sometimes stayed for lunch at school we usually went home regardless of distance, but we did have an hour and a half. For the school lunches we descended into a very cramped diningroom in the boarding house basement, where we sat on benches so tightly packed that it was impossible to move ones elbows which certainly made eating into quite an art!

This house was on a steep slope and so the basement was light and led out into the tarmacced garden playground at the back, from which steps led on down into another larger walled garden. Sometimes in the summer we sat in this garden for 'sewing' while someone read aloud to us, later it was turned into tennis courts and today it has become a car park.

For any extra activities like games and swimming we went out, there was hockey on Saturday mornings in the winter, played on the large fields off Combe Road, now lost, completely built over by the R.U.H. and car parks. Tennis on summer afternoons, when we used the courts behind the Lansdown Grove Hotel, walking up and down the steep little pathway known as 'The Shrubbery' and across Lansdown Road.

For swimming, in the early days we used the large bath attached to the medical centre at the Pump Room Hotel. It was a rather strange bath, all one depth and no diving boards, just shallow steps the whole length of one side with a blank wall opposite attached to which was a long brass rail to hold on to. This often got us into trouble because it was so easy to hang on to that rail with our backs to the mistress in charge on the far side and pretend not to hear her increasingly desperate calls to 'come out at once'!

Very soon however the 'New Baths' were opened further down the town complete with diving boards, deep and shallow ends, proper changing rooms and a small balcony above one end where parents could sit and watch our efforts, and we moved on.

In a ragged chattering crocodile, with our bathing dresses and towels rolled up under our arms we marched off, down little Saville Row on down Milsom Street and passed the Cross Bath which was free, noisy and very popular: to the 'new bath'.

A Mr. Marsh was our instructor, he was a good and patient teacher who somehow managed to get us through all the various tests from bronze to gold, as well as our Girl Guide swimming badges on the way.

We plunged, dived and swam lengths on our backs and fronts, rescued each other from certain death by drowning while fully clothed and dived to collect as many tin plates from the bottom as could be managed in one breath clasping them desperately to our chests as we came gasping up to the surface. For the Guide badge it was copper pennies, much larger than today's' pennies but still difficult to pick up from the tiled bottom of the pool.

The examiner for all these tests was a Swiss, Monsieur Meyer who owned a popular little Swiss café on the corner of New Bond Street and the passageway running through to Upper Boro Walls and The Corridor, which was our favourite meeting place on Saturday mornings.

We sat at small marble topped tables to drink hot chocolate topped with cream and slices of a feather light sponge cake filled with fresh cream and topped with soft dark chocolate icing.

His wife Madame Meyer owned a bakery and a larger Swiss café 'The Bernina' in Old Bond Street and a patisserie where she made those delicious cakes. The plate glass window came right down to pavement level and was filled with baskets of fresh croissants and brioche, guarded by a life sized carved wooden bear standing on his hind legs on one side and a large wooden Swiss chalet on the other.

At sometime around my eleventh birthday the Miss Websters retired and the two new owners moved the school a short distance up the hill into the centre houses of Portland Place. This was an enormous improvement in every way, the buildings had previously held a school and were spacious and well equipped, with a large assembly hall combined with a gym, and proper cloakrooms, no more dark, damp basement.

The classrooms were large and light although we still had our old desks, battered and ink stained, each one with a china inkwell in the top right hand corner, kept filled daily by an 'ink orderly'. We became quite fond of our desks, they were very personal, the hinged lids lifted up, this was useful when one needed to pass on information or remarks unseen by the mistress in charge.

Inside our desks we kept absolutely everything from exercise books and text books to pin ups cut out from magazines, and comics, the occasional bar of chocolate or packet of sucky sweets, no chewing gum in those days or even packets of crisps, if there had been we would certainly have had them. All we had to carry home in a satchel or bicycle basket would be the necessary books for our homework, everything else stayed at school in our desks.

Quite a number of activities went on outside the school itself besides games and swimming. Those of us who showed any special interest in 'art' went down to the Bath School of Art in the Guildhall once a week where all I remember is sitting on tiered benches with large drawing boards in front of us to draw various arrangements of white plaster cubes, tubes and pyramids and blue paper sugar bags.

Until the school moved up to Portland Place which had an assembly hall equipped as a gymnasium, we walked the short distance along Julian Road and down Guinea Lane to the Paragon where the Olsens, a Swedish husband and wife had their gym. We loved our gym days, climbing up ropes to the ceiling and hanging up there like monkeys, balancing on or vaulting over beams, I found vaulting over a five barred gate no problem until I was well on in years thanks to Captain Olsen, and were sad when we changed over to our own gym mistress at the school.

For exams like the annual School Certificate those of us who were sitting them went off down to the Guildhall again, this was quite popular because we could go out during the lunch break to a little café on the nearby Pultney Bridge and look out of the window straight down to the river and weir below.

Dancing Class

F ROM A VERY EARLY AGE we went to a dancing class, Wednesday afternoon was for 'dancing', there were two rival schools, Miss Chart and Miss Woodhead-Smith.

Jean, Ruth and I went to Miss Chart's held in a large upstairs room in one of the houses on the high pavement in George Street above what is now the 'Hole in the Wall' restaurant. (It was a coal cellar in those days!)

A light room with big windows looking down on to the street with a highly polished floor and a pianist at an upright piano in one corner, and chairs against the wall for mothers and nannies. We came dressed in pretty party frocks carrying our slippers in a cotton shoe bag, bronze or black dancing slippers similar to ballet shoes were de rigueur and always

Pulteney Bridge and the Weir

worn for parties as well. We had short silk socks and the shoes fastened round our ankles with criss crossing elastic. Under our dresses we all wore white petticoats with tucks and lace edgings, it was important to have a pocket in one's petticoat not as far as we were concerned for a hankie, but somewhere to put one's treasures at parties, pictures off the crackers, little trinkets and any small gift or prize from games to be taken home.

Dancing classes continued right up to the time we left school.

The High Pavement in George Street

In the early days there were a few small boys, and much later some of the older boys joined us at the beginning of each Christmas holidays so that they could learn to dance with a partner and the latest dance steps, ready for the parties and dances during the holidays, it was a sensible idea and saved us all a lot of grief!

But back to our regular dancing classes, with our shoes changed and hair tidied we were ready to begin, the pianist would play an introductory cord or two and we sorted ourselves out into lines, the girls all curtsied to Miss Chart and the boys bowed low. Exercises first with much emphasis on the pointing of toes, some skipping to music which was fun, and then into dances proper.

There were 'Sir Roger de Coverley' and 'Strip the Willow' because we were certain to have these at some of the parties and then ballroom dancing. Miss Chart may have been strict but she understood children, we began with the more difficult and to us dull dances, the 'waltz' and the 'foxtrot' and on to the 'polka', 'one, two, three and turn, one, two, three and turn' which was more fun but liable to get out of control, and finally we were able to really let off steam with an extremely boisterous gallop and it was over for another week.

Brownies and Guides

A ROUND OUR EIGHTH BIRTHDAYS we discovered the Brownies, the school had a Brownie Pack and a Girl Guide Company, and some of our happiest memories must be of the time we spent as Brownies and Guides.

My own memories of the Brownie days, apart from two events, are not very clear, it is after all a very long time ago!

We were divided into 'Sixes' each with a leader a 'Sixer', I do not think that we ever rose to that exalted height, we did better in the Guides. Jean was a Pixie 'helping people when in fixes' and I was an Elf 'think of

The Brownie pack, seated left to right: Ruth, Jean and Angie

others not ourselves'. There was a much loved 'Brown Owl' and we danced round a bright red toadstool singing our little jingles, and I think that we worked quite hard to gain some badges. For one of them we had to make a rice pudding, which probably was much harder than it sounds, and all the milk ran out of mine in my bicycle basket as I carried it to school for the judging but I think it passed the test in spite of being rather dry.

The other very clear memory is of an exciting picnic to the top of Combe Down. We gathered outside the school wearing our well ironed brown uniforms and bright yellow ties, shoes and little dancing Brownie badges shining, and off we went with Brown Owl an excited chattering little crowd down into the town to catch the tram.

The trams climbed all the way to the top of Combe Down to the 'Glass House'. The Glass House, although it had a small café and rather disappointingly was not made of glass, was better known as the terminal where the trams either returned down the hill to the city or branched off to run the entire length of the top of Combe Down as far as what is today Bath University, our destination.

Here we spent the day in a large field and among a small copse of beech trees (I think that the beech trees are still there). We played games and ate our picnic and generally ran wild and at the end of the day climbed back on to another tram to return home, it had been an exciting day.

At eleven years old we left the undemanding world of the Brownies and with a small ceremony were welcomed into the Guide Company, here there were 'Patrols' instead of 'Sixes' each with a Leader and a Second, Jean became a 'Thistle' and I was a 'Fuchsia'.

The Guides suited us perfectly with a delightful Captain, a Miss Balm known always as 'Balmy', and a wide variety of things to learn and do and much fun and laughter.

The highlight was the annual Camp, we had never camped before and so our first was especially exciting. The great day finally arrived and

Guide camp, the bell tents, Jean and Deirdre

we all gathered on the steps outside the school to board the bus which was to take us out to the Camp site at Winsley, in a field just below the sanatorium.

Big old-fashioned bell tents with their central poles and dozens of large wooden tent pegs to hold them steady were to be our 'home' for the next ten days. A patrol to a tent, we slept feet to the centre on palliases filled with straw, our belongings packed into knapsacks as pillows. Much ingenuity was called for to make useful gadgets, a rack of sticks for shoes, or a small table if a suitable piece of flat wood could be found, it was important to keep your tent as tidy and attractive as possible, there was a daily inspection and much competition. Although we had torches it was more fun to collect several of the small glow worms from the surrounding grass and put them into an empty jam jar and use them as a lamp, there were plenty of glow worms around in those days and they could be released the next day.

Of course we all brought a good supply of things like biscuits and sweets which were shared around usually at night, but far and away the most popular were the packets of chocolate coated raisins belonging to Deirdre. Deirdre was a vegetarian which in those days was unusual and considered, certainly by us as rather odd, and I am ashamed to say that most of her precious raisins were eaten by the rest of us.

We continued to be a source of trouble none of it really serious, but the school found it hard to devise punishments which had any lasting effect until one day the Head Mistress hit on the idea of punishing us via the Guides. I have no idea what we had done, probably we had failed to come out of the swimming pool when called and so had held up everyone else, the punishment was quite ingenious.

By this time we were both Patrol Leaders with two white tape stripes on our top left hand pockets, we were told to come to school wearing our Guide uniforms and at morning assembly were called out to the front, where after a short speech explaining our offence the Head Mistress cut off our white stripes with a pair of scissors!

I doubt if it had any lasting effect, and we were soon re-installed by 'Balmy' who was a wise person who understood children and was not a part of the school.

Jean continued in the Guides going on to become a Ranger, the senior branch and gaining something exalted called 'all round cords', while I joined another company at boarding school and became a 'skylark' a much more suitable name than 'fuchsia'!

Holidays and Times out of School

A LTHOUGH I REMEMBER much of what went on at school, it is the holidays and times out of school hours that I remember best. Our school holidays were much longer with a whole month at Christmas and Easter and two in the summer, and with no television or computers every child spent more time out of doors whatever the weather no 'couch potatoes' in those days and the very occasional fat child had a pretty tough time of it.

Bath was and I am sure that it still is a wonderful place in which to grow up and thankfully we were totally unaware of how unbelievably few were to be the years between the two great wars, only twenty one years from 1918 the end of the first to 1939 the start of the second.

With Jean then living in St. James' Square, Angie in Park Lane and Ruth in the Newbridge Road we were all heading in the same direction and once released from school, especially during the lunch hour, freedom went to our heads and although we always managed to get home for some lunch eventually, there were a great many distractions on the way.

Both the school and our parents devised various schemes aimed at getting us straight home, none of them succeeded, one of the senior prefects lived in Weston Park and was given the hopeless task of escorting each of us right to our gates, we just turned round and met up again usually in Victoria Park. Another idea was a card signed by a mistress with the time we left school to be counter signed by a parent on arrival home, that failed because in the rush at home it was often lost or forgotten, and there were of course a variety of punishments, eventually I suppose we grew out of it and both Ruth and Angie departed to boarding school.

Having bumped our way from the school in Portland Place down the cobbles of Burlington Street, short but steep, we were in Julian Road which runs from Lansdown Road opposite Guinea Lane passed St. Andrew's Church to the entrance to St. James' Square, we always thought that it was called Julian because it was on the site of a Roman road, perhaps it was?

This is where the distractions began, Bath has a number of wide raised pavements, the Paragon where Captain Olsen had his gym is one of the longest, and just above the old Ear, Nose and Throat Hospital on the corner of Lansdown Road was another. Here the little newsagent tobacconist and sweet shop sold our favourite toffees, 'Sharps Super Kreemy Toffees', delicious individually wrapped really creamy toffees sold from large tins with their trademark picture on the lid, a dapper little man with an eye glass and a parrot. They also had the tiny little Frys chocolate creams, excellent for dolls tea parties, these were the ones which we were given after drinking my Mother's horrible tasting cough medicine, everything was sold loose by weight usually in small cone shaped white paper bags, this shop was a little off our usual 'beat'.

On our way home we had to pass several interesting shops on the high pavement opposite St. Andrew's church. There was one which sold a wide selection of religious things, bibles and prayer books as well as statues of the Madonna and crucifixes, etc. Our visits were not to buy any of these things but to sort through the several flat baskets on the counter which were filled with small items including little china jugs and mugs in dolls house sizes, costing only a penny or so each, the kind and patient lady behind the counter let us spend as long as we liked before finally handing over our pennies. Considering how long ago that was, eighty or so years, it is surprising how many of those little jugs and mugs are still hanging from the dresser in the same old dolls house.

That little shop also sold the white clay pipes which we used to blow bubbles from a small bowl of soapy water, and do not ever make the mistake of sucking in when taking a fresh breath or you will get a mouth full of soap!

The last shop before St. James' Square, still on the high pavement, was the dairy with a beautiful white china swan in the window, which I only visited very occasionally with my mother. Inside was all cool white tiles with a wide well scrubbed slate counter. Standing on this counter would be several large white china bowls, one contained eggs white ones, brown ones and all shades in between, another was filled with fresh cool milk together with several small copper measures hanging from the side, a gill, a half pint etc., and two slightly smaller bowls one with raw cream as it was called, no fuss over pasteurising in those days, and the other golden crusty clotted cream. A visit to the dairy usually meant the treat of a large glass of ice cold milk with 'a gill of cream please' added, absolutely delicious.

Round the corner in St. James' Square were several food shops, a butcher whose open fronted shop was built into the archway, not of any interest, but next door was Ifoulds the grocers which was where my mother did her shopping, owned and run by Mr. and Mrs Ifould always a very profitable and popular port of call. The shop was divided into two with a connecting door. Mr. Ifould presided over the cheese and bacon and hams section with the usual wide mahogany counter and several chairs for the customers to use while giving their order, assistants did all the searching and fetching and carrying, how much easier than today's trailing round a supermarket with a trolley and then queuing at the 'cash out'.

Kind Mrs. Ifould was in charge of the much more interesting things like cakes, and biscuits and sweets.

Because most things were sold loose by the pound from large tins or boxes or big glass jars, there were often broken biscuits or odd or damaged chocolate bars or chocolates and these were sold off to eager children with very limited pocket money, a halfpenny worth of 'bust choc' as we called it was a real treasure, and Mrs. Ifould would sometimes add a few whole biscuits we never knew what to discover in our small paper bags.

Off we would go on our bikes into Victoria Park usually to climb over or through the railings into 'Robin Hoods Dell' at the Weston Park end, a favourite place where we spent many happy hours hidden among the trees and shrubs, all the more popular because it was forbidden territory. Once when trying to eat a toffee from one of Mrs. Ifoulds paper bags Honor had difficulty with her 'plate', both Honor and I wore uncomfortable 'braces' to straighten our teeth, so she removed hers and hid it up a tree, unfortunately when it came to the time to go home we had forgotten which tree and failed to find it, plates being expensive things she got into considerable trouble.

Skating

E VERY YEAR SOMETIME AFTER CHRISTMAS there would come the cold weather, cold enough to freeze the lakes and ponds, and then the water-meadows would be flooded to make out door skating rinks; at night more water would be let in to give a fresh smooth surface for the next day, and often there were boys anxious to earn a few pennies who kept them swept by day.

In Bath the water meadows were at the back of the houses along the London road beyond the Cleveland Bridge, and sometimes we were taken out to the Midford meadows below the

Mill which were not so crowded.

As soon as the news spread that the meadows were frozen out would come the skates, it was all great fun and exciting. There were skates of every kind from home made strips of polished metal

screwed or tied on to every day boots to elegant continental skates attached to laced up skating boots.

Usually there were a few old men with a kitchen chair who would help put on and lace up boots, or hire out the chair to support unsteady beginners for a few coppers.

There would be glowing hot braziers roasting chestnuts and good for warming cold hands, sometimes music and after dark flares were lit so that skating could go on until late at night.

Today's organised indoor skating rinks cannot compare with the fun and exhilaration of those impromptu out door 'rinks' in the cold frosty weather. Whole families and all ages joined in from boys just sliding and bumping to elderly gentlemen showing considerable skill

skating elegantly round hands behind their backs, rosy cheeked ladies cutting beautiful figures of eight and couples hands crossed skating together in perfect time. There were fathers holding up giggling, squealing children and beginners clinging to the edges falling down and getting up laughing to start all over again, everyone enjoyed themselves, it was a much looked forward to part of every winter.

Parties

T HE BEAUTIFUL OLD HOUSES in the Circus and Crescents, all of them still family homes and not yet divided up into flats, were perfect for parties and small dances. Most had an upstairs drawing room some with large doors which folded back into an adjoining room, the floors were of polished wood with loose carpets easily rolled back, and almost all would have a grand piano and someone able to play it for dancing or musical games.

Christmas was the most popular time for parties, although I do not think that we were great party goers! Little girls would wear their prettiest dresses (with a petticoat of course) and bronze dancing slippers, and would arrive carrying their slippers in a small shoe bag, most of us having walked from home or travelled on the tram.

Parties usually followed a pattern which would have been familiar to our parents and even grandparents, and occasionally there would be a conjuror. We played 'Hunt the slipper', 'Blind Man's buff', and 'I sent a letter to my love', and usually one or two singing games, 'Here we come gathering nuts in May' and 'Oranges and Lemons' which not only taught us the names of the City of London churches but ended with the rather frightening 'here comes a candle to light you to bed and here comes a chopper to chop off your head, chop, chop, chop, CHOP and down would come the encircling arms of the two people making the arch under which we had to run. I have often wondered how far back in our history does that go, we surely have not chopped off heads for a very long time?

When we grew out of the more childish games we would take partners and line up facing each other to dance 'Sir Roger de Coverley', a traditional country dance, and just to write the name I find myself humming the repetitive little tune.

We didn't expect or receive expensive prizes or presents and went home happy with small trinkets from the crackers and perhaps a bar of chocolate as a prize.

Various Events

The General Strike

T HE GENERAL STRIKE in 1926, although it was obviously a very serious event did not mean much to us as children, we just thought that it was all rather exciting and fun.

The few trains which ran were manned and driven by volunteers, mostly students, and these of course included some of our friend's older brothers. So off we would go down to the station, it must have been during our school holidays, to wait for their arrival and cheer them on their way, it was all very light hearted because of course those young men also thought it great fun!

The Secret Garden

O NE OTHER THING HAPPENED which affected the two of us as a direct result of the strike, but really had nothing to do with it.

The high wall surrounding the Richmond House garden had a rounded top, and in one of the disused stables we found an old leather saddle and by standing on a box we could put it over the top of the wall and sitting astride pretend it was a galloping horse. We were Cavaliers and the passers-by, more of them than usual because of the lack of buses and trams, were Roundheads to be challenged.

One of them stopped to talk and I can only suppose that we were quite a polite and friendly pair obviously using our imaginations and enjoying our game, anyway Mrs. King for that was her name, invited us to go and play in her garden which was just across the road from our stable yard, at any time we liked, no need to call at the house just go in.

It was an absolutely wonderful invitation which transformed our lives. Of course there were the large cultivated gardens but for us the joy was several acres of hayfield with a stream running through the bottom and small woodlands.

We spent hours and hours playing in the stream and among the buttercups and wild flowers and looking for birds nests, I remember discovering a long tailed tits nest and watching from eggs to fledglings, being fascinated by the way the mother bird folded her long tail back over her head in the tiny domed nest.

At Christmas one year Mrs. King gave us a book 'The Secret Garden' by Mrs. Hodgson Burnett, inscribed inside 'To the two little girls who love another secret garden'. Jean has that book on her shelf of special books to this day, I already had a copy.

I think that the Kings loved children but had none of their own, we hardly ever saw them to talk to although I am quite sure that they knew when we were there, I hope that we gave them half as much pleasure as their garden gave us.

The Legion Fair

A HIGHLIGHT OF EVERY SUMMER was the Legion Fair held in the large upper field in Victoria Park which we had to pass every day as we bicycled to and from school. Many were the hours we spent watching the familiar attractions being set up and wandering around among the stalls and fairground caravans, entrance was free and open to everyone.

I think that we were all less sophisticated in those days, we did not need to be scared stiff on giant roller coasters or things which turn you upside down at speed, although all the colour and noise were the same and just as much fun. And because no one travelled far or moved around so much, a fair was quite a major excitement and the ground was packed every day from the time it opened in the afternoon until late at night.

As at every fair the largest and noisiest attraction was the big roundabout with its galloping horses and highly polished 'barley sugar' twisted brass poles, belting out all the popular music from its hurdy-gurdy organ at the centre, brightly lit at night everyone loved to ride on the roundabout.

There were swing boats and coconut shies, shooting galleries, boxing rings and fortune-tellers in tents, gold fishes to be won on the hooplas and a smaller roundabout with swings on long chains which swung out almost parallel with the ground as it gathered speed, with only a small chain across the tummy to hold you in. I do not think that we ever really enjoyed it and certainly never went on one again after a very frightening experience when the safety chain on the swing in front of us broke at the fastest stage and the girl in it fell head first to be caught by one foot in the chains. The roundabout was only able to stop quite slowly and she continued to swing head down screaming loudly until someone was able to run round supporting her until it stopped, she was not hurt but badly frightened and so were we!

Our favourite of all for which we saved up our precious pocket money was the 'Cake Walk', you climbed up some steps on to a sort of bridge which jolted up and down doing its best to throw you down as you battled your way to the far end, there was no time limit (perhaps that was its attraction) we loved it and stayed on as long as possible.

We visited that fair every day even when our money had run out and enjoyed every moment.

There were two other events in Bath's summer calendar at which we would love to have spent as much time had they both been nearer to home and not needing official entry tickets which we could not afford. They were the Bath and West Agricultural Show and the annual Bath Horse Show.

In those long ago days the 'Bath and West' as it is always known, had no permanent show ground and moved round the region visiting a different town each year and only came to Bath occasionally. The one which I remember was held on the top of Rushill where there was still plenty of open field space, a smaller show than today's but still a great deal larger and more prestigious than the small local ones.

The big main show ring had no stands or permanent buildings but was surrounded by chairs, benches and straw bales, there were the same parades and judging of beautiful animals, bands played and the local hunts paraded their hounds to great acclaim.

'Walls' who were the main makers of ice cream, sold cornets and 'wafers', a thick slab of ice cream between two wafers, there were toffee apples and popcorn and presumably other more substantial things to eat which were not of any interest to the children, a wonderful day out.

The Horse Show took place over several days on the old Horse Show ground at Lambridge out towards Batheaston, this was its own ground with permanent stands and stabling and was used in the winter as a rugger pitch. Although I think the shows ceased with the second world war, the local guides and maps continued to show 'Horse Show Ground' until very recently when it finally vanished under the by-pass and giant roundabout.

Bath's annual Horse Show was a big event in the horsey world, there were none of the Badmintons and Burleighs at which to show off your skills and horses, it was a great day devoted entirely to horses. You must remember that the horse was still in every day use, pulling tradesmen's carts, farm wagons and ploughs, in the forests and pulling heavily laden barges along the much used network of canals and so the show was of great interest to everyone. It was still a common sight to see a labourer going to and from work sitting sideways on the broad back of his great heavy horse, leading another. We loved the Horse Show and usually managed to visit it several times.

Bicycles and Freedom

P ONIES MUST HAVE GIVEN the generations before us freedom to roam and discover the world around them and of course to visit friends, they must have loved their ponies those who were lucky enough to have one.

For us it was bicycles, most of us owned a bike of some sort Jean's was a hand down from her brother, a boys bike with a crossbar, mine a

fairly new girl's one. We had metal 'carriers' over our rear wheels and a wicker basket in front attached to the handlebars with two small straps, and hand brakes which required fairly frequent visits to the bicycle shop on the corner of St. James's Square, for new blocks (Bath is all hills up and down), no gears we just had to pedal extra hard.

How lucky we were with so much freedom, allowed to go wherever we liked, no mobile phones so no contact, any problems, and of course there were problems - times have not changed all that much - we learned to cope with ourselves.

There was another very close friend with whom I grew up as well as Jean, Honor, the granddaughter of Sir Isaac Pitman the inventor of shorthand. We were exactly the same age, only two weeks separating our birthdays.

Honor was the youngest and only girl in a large family of boys, Jim, Chris, Jack and Peter who was the nearest in age. With lessons at home with a governess she had fewer friends of her own age, so I was welcomed by her family. Their home 'Penn Hill' is a big house in spreading grounds about mid-way along the then small lane between Upper Weston village and the Kelston road. I must have bicycled the two or three miles between our homes

hundreds of times from the age of about nine, often calling in on the sweet shop at the crossroads, a dark little shop down a short flight of steps with a bow window and rows of glass jars of sweets, tangerine balls were our favourites, the shop sold all sorts of other things, I remember buying a very special present for my mother one day, a small aluminium tin of brilliant pink tooth powder, I don't remember her reaction!

What a wonderful place in which to grow up, 'Penn' had everything one could want, unlimited freedom, ponies and stables, dogs and a black cat called 'Lucky' who lived in the kitchen and had endless litters of kittens in the bottom cupboard of the kitchen dresser.

There were gardens with trees and lawns where we played 'hide and seek', 'kick the can' and bicycle polo. One huge old elm tree had a tree house reached via a long rope ladder, it was quite high up, I have always been a coward and although I was quite happy to climb the rope which hung alongside (shades of Captain Olsen and his gym) I was never brave enough to climb that swaying ladder.

Tennis courts and a paddock with jumps for riding the ponies.

In the vegetable garden there was a net covered strawberry bed under which we would crawl to stuff ourselves with the fat juicy strawberries while lying in the warm straw under a hot summer sun, and no gardener ever came to scold and stop us.

The house itself was a spacious family home, upstairs there was the nursery with its own small kitchen and bathroom where nanny had presided until being replaced by the governess, here we sometimes had our tea, although we usually came down to the drawing room to join any visitors and the rest of the family.

Apart from having to be tidy and polite and 'handing round', children were not kept shut away in the Pitman home, all I can remember is that there were tiny sandwiches and hot buttered toast with 'Gentlemen's Relish' which I did not like, and always a large plate with a cleverly stacked pyramid of Bourbon biscuits, I can never see a Bourbon biscuit without being taken straight back to those Penn Hill teas.

The big dining room had a very long table, they were a large family and there were usually friends as well, with heavy green leather seated chairs, the leather was cold and tended to stick to bare legs, Mrs. Pitman sat at one end and Mr. Pitman at the other.

Round the walls were large family portraits with an almost life sized one of Honor behind Mrs. Pitman, probably painted when she was about eight years old, wearing a black velvet dress with a champagne coloured lace collar and cuffs.

I was often there for a family lunch, happy occasions but strict table manners and behaviour, I shall never forget the day when I tipped my big chair on to its back legs and Mrs. Pitman brought both her hands down on to the table with such a crash that not only I but everything on the table jumped as she shouted at me 'never let me see you do that again'. and my goodness I never have!

At one end of the ground floor was the old billiard room with a door leading out into the garden which was the way we usually came in and out, the table had gone which left plenty of space for roller skating on wet days. The room was also a useful dump for all sorts of discarded odds and ends including a large galvanised tin bath.

There was a good deal of showing off and daring when the three of us were together, for Jean was often there as well, and one day when we were playing in one of the loose boxes with her pony the dare was to somersault off her pony's bare back.

I watched both Jean and Honor somersault over the long suffering pony's tail to land on the hard stable floor and wind themselves and knew that I was not brave enough, I could not do it. Instead I was led back into the billiard room where I had to do various tricks on the stilts, on which I will admit we were quite well practised, the worst and most difficult was to step from the hard polished floor into the tin bath and out again on the other side, it required very careful balance and was very nerve wracking but I did it, anything was better than the stable floor!

Our lives continued happily and companionably bicycling to and from each other's homes for the next few years until suddenly just before Honor and I had our fourteenth birthdays we were packed off to boarding school, Honor as one of the very first pupils at the then new Westonbirt School, and me to near London to Parkfield in Potters Bar, while lucky Jean stayed on at the Hermitage House. Let no one tell you that the start of boarding school is not traumatic, it is very, but it usually ends up happily.

We all remained at school until we were eighteen, for me that was in 1930 and although we continued to get together during the holidays nothing seems to have made any impression until we were in our last year and around seventeen.

When during those last school holidays Honor began to learn to fly from the Flying School at Filton, an unusual thing for a girl in those days and considered very dashing.

While I learned to drive my Grandfather's heavy old Armstrong Siddeley car with Beecham the rather dour elderly chauffeur, we circled Victoria Park round and round until I had mastered the difficult art of double de-clutching, before progressing out to the Viaduct Hotel to face the horror of Brass Knocker Hill.

Stalling that heavy old car with all the complication of brakes and gears and double de-clutching was no joke, especially as self starters did not exist and every car had to be cranked up with a starting handle which often took several swings, thankfully Beecham did the cranking while I held desperately on to the brakes.

Once Beecham considered that I could drive reasonably well all I had to do was go to the Post Office with £5 and fill in a form to be given my Driving Licence, no such thing as a test!

The Shops

S HOPS AND SHOPPING have always been one of Bath's attractions and although the beautiful individually owned shops for which the City was renowned have all gone, and the changes came gradually, they have altered the Bath of my childhood for ever.

Almost all the most prestigious shops were in Milsom Street, one exception being Mallorys the jewellers on the corner of Bridge Street and they are the sole survivors, still owned by the same family today. The shop itself is unchanged, the upper half a treasure house of jewellery and precious objects in silver and gold, and the lower selling glass and china. Mallorys was where we came for my engagement ring and later on for wedding presents.

Here Bath buns and chocolate Olivers enter the story because the first shop that I am going to describe is 'Fortts' the bakers and confectioners at the bottom right hand side of Milsom Street with a handsome royal coat of arms over the main entrance.

The coat of arms has long since been removed and Fortts is no more, the whole shop and the restaurant at the back has closed and today there is a bookshop, a part of the large Waterstones chain.

Fortts was a rather grand establishment with a marble floored shop which sold breads and rolls and delicious mouth watering cream cakes, as well as expensive handmade chocolates. Their speciality was the Bath bun, perhaps the royal family were fond of Bath buns and Fortts supplied the palace, hence the royal coat of arms, buns by appointment!

Fortts premises in Milsom Street, now Waterstones

A real Bath bun is very special, round and flattish, a deep saffron gold in colour, sweet and a little spicy with a glazed sugar top sprinkled with tiny pieces of cane sugar and currants, and at the centre of every bun was a whole lump of sugar which became crunchy when baked. Sadly today buns which call themselves Bath buns are made all over the country and are a pale shadow of the real thing with no lump of sugar!

Fortts was much more than just a shop, at the back was a large restaurant which was a popular place for morning coffee and afternoon tea. Just inside the entrance on the left-hand side was a small alcove with a palm filled stage where three elderly ladies in long black dresses sat and played soothing music on piano, violin and cello.

A visit to Fortts for coffee when shopping was almost obligatory and for the children there would be hot chocolate with a blob of cream or an ice cream in a small glass dish, and always a plate of 'chocolate Olivers'.

'Chocolate Olivers' are very unusual biscuits. In about 1735 a Doctor Oliver who lived in Bath began to make a plain hard biscuit which goes excellently with Stilton cheese, they became very popular and he started a factory in a red brick building down by the Great Western Railway station, where there was a large portrait of Dr Oliver's head on the front wall; every biscuit also has his head in the centre, his trade mark. Sometime later he tried dipping those plain hard biscuits into thick dark plain chocolate, the combination of the hard unsweetened biscuit with the thick covering of plain chocolate is unique and delicious and both varieties are now sold all over the world. The factory in Bath has gone but Bath Olivers are still made to the original recipe by several of the large biscuit makers.

Above the restaurant was a large ballroom which was popular for parties, dances and even the occasional Hunt ball, Fortts was an important centre of Bath's social life.

On the other side of the street was 'Charles' the shoe shop, the entrance set back from the pavement lined with glass show case windows while inside were deep piled carpets and comfortable benches and chairs. Once when my mother was choosing a pair of shoes I was given a present of a shoe horn, no ordinary shoe horn but one which I kept and treasured for many years made of a plastic bright with every colour of the rainbow, beautiful!

The children's' department was at the back of the shop where the annual ritual of buying new shoes took place. In the autumn there would be a pair of stout brown lace up leather shoes for out of doors, and a new pair of indoor shoes brown with a bar fastening made by Clarks which went by the name of 'Every whens'.

Every Easter holidays summer was ushered in with a new pair of sandals, dancing slippers in bronze must have appeared at sometime but they do not seem to have made any impression. We did not have Gumboots or Wellington boots instead galoshes in shiny brown or black were a useful substitute, they just slipped over ones indoor shoes.

Further down on the bottom left hand side on the corner there was, and still is, Lloyds Bank, and on the opposite corner of Green Street 'Liptons' the grocers. I can just remember standing here in a long queue with Grannie Scott for some ham, there was rationing in the 1914-18 war and ham was probably a luxury in short supply, it seems to have made a big impression.

Higher up the street, still on the left-hand side was 'Mallets' the antique shop a great favourite with Queen Mary. We would often see her arrive in her large Daimler car wearing a toque and carrying her umbrella, to be ushered in to browse among the furniture and beautiful objects. No trouble with massed photographers and the only visible sign of security the occasional single policeman.

Further down still on the left-hand side were 'Lords' the tailors, who made everything from uniforms and hunting clothes to court dress and tailcoats. The shop was filled with bolts of cloth and tweeds of every description and elderly assistants with tape measures hanging round their necks who must have handed down their skills from father to son over several generations to make clothes for the succeeding generations of families from the surrounding countryside.

They even condescended to tailor for ladies and my very first coat and skirt was made by Lords and cost all of £8.

Near the top right hand side of Milsom Street there was a 'Fullers' cake and tea shop much smaller than Fortts, Fullers had branches in London and most of the larger towns, they were famous for their very special white sugar iced walnut cakes, mention Fullers to anyone who remembers their shops and the first thing they will say is 'oh walnut cakes'!

With Fortts at the lower end and Fullers near the top, most of the rest of that side of the street was filled by 'Jollys', there was also a branch of Jollys in Clifton the more fashionable part of Bristol. Although Jollys is still there in name it is now a part of a vast chain of shops.

There are three entrances from Milsom Street the centre one a wide marble and pillared affair, Jollys was a really lovely shop filled with expensive and beautiful things from clothes to furniture. There was a delicious department selling cosmetics with a glass counter and shelves of the most expensive soaps and perfumes, with elegant and to a child, rather disdainful ladies serving behind that glass counter.

The millinery department was presided over by a tall very dignified lady called Miss Hulbert and was divided into two sections, the outer was for the lesser mortals and sold the less expensive hats, while the inner sanctum which was circular and contained special creations and the most expensive hats was Miss Hulbert's exclusive domain from which she seldom emerged. We were all rather in awe of Miss H and never ventured beyond the open doorway, I don't think I ever went inside until I was to be a bridesmaid and very much later as a bride, weddings were her speciality.

The children's department was separate and could be entered from the lowest of the three entrances, a happy department in charge of two delightful ladies who loved and understood children, Miss Target, known to us all as 'Targie' and Miss Ryder, 'Targie' was short and plump and Miss Ryder tall and thin. The department sold everything from Chilprufe vests and 'combinations' to silk party socks. There were very few ready made clothes, but as materials were not at all expensive and 'Targie' was an excellent dressmaker and tailor most things were made to order. And much later because we had been 'her children' she was also allowed by the more senior dressmakers, to make our wedding and bridesmaid's dresses which was a great concession. This involved much ritual and ceremony in special fitting rooms whose dividing double doors were thrown open, sheets spread on the floor and chairs for visitors, mothers and friends and was a lot of fun.

The department which sold linens and materials by the yard was always a favourite, with a very long wide polished mahogany counter and several high chairs for the customers to sit on while viewing and choosing. In charge was a cheerful, friendly gentleman with several assistants who did most of the fetching and carrying of the heavy rolls of materials, I cannot remember his name but think it was Lane, he was always addressed very formally as Mr. Lane.

Mr. Lane had a small cubby hole at one end of the counter, a miniature office where he dealt with the orders and cash, sometimes we would be allowed behind the counter to be given small pieces of materials, lovely coloured silks and flowery cottons, and on one never to be forgotten occasion I was handed six tiny white linen towels all beautifully hemstitched for my dolls house. They were a travellers sample and unwanted, but not by me, although they were so small they were real towels to be treasured and after countless washings and ironings by a succession of busy little girls, I have them still hanging on a little brass towel rail in the bedroom of my mother's old dolls house.

Away from Milsom Street there were plenty of other shops, there was 'Theobalds' in little Old Bond Street almost next door to Madame Myer's 'Bernina' café, always filled with the delicious aroma of freshly roasted coffee from the wonderful old green painted barrel shaped roaster which seemed to be tossing and roasting coffee beans all day long.

Whenever Aunt Mabel took us out it was always to Theobalds, this was her firm favourite, although we didn't drink coffee, I think it must have been popular with connoisseurs of real good fresh coffee.

Supermarkets had not yet been invented instead there were the much more convenient and friendly smaller shops scattered about all round the city, grocers, bakers, fishmongers, butchers and greengrocers. Little Green Street for example running between the bottom of Milsom Street and Broad Street had everything you needed, from Liptons the grocer and Lloyds Bank at one end to a small branch of Fortts at the other. In between was a splendid mix, a butcher, fishmonger, greengrocer and a wonderful old fashioned bookshop, 'Gregorys' and another which I think was called a furriers, a fur shop, selling all sorts of furs and fur coats, lovely and warm and beautiful to look at, no protesters in those days!

Even the children often had a fur coat, mine was grey squirrel with a ridiculous hat to match which had a little lace frill all round the edge (see frontispiece).

'Cater, Stoffel and Fortt' always known as 'Caters', were the largest grocers, in the High Street almost opposite the Guildhall they were very like Harrods food halls, if you couldn't get it at Caters you were unlikely to find it anywhere else in Bath.

There were great hams and sides of bacon to be sliced while you watched, big round cheeses Stiltons and Cheddars nothing foreign in those days, and teas and sugars sold loose by the pound, sugar for some reason was always packed into special thick blue paper bags. Dundee marmalade was sold in straight sided beige coloured earthenware jars with Dundee written on the side in large black letters. Nothing was pre-packed in dull sealed packets, you were able to buy as much or as little as you needed, the big square tins of biscuits were displayed with their lids off tilted forward so that you were able to chose exactly what you liked and when in doubt would be allowed to taste a sample.

On the right hand side of Bond Street about half way down was 'The Red House' another baker and cake shop, which also had a restaurant immediately behind the shop, I think that this one, which was entered up four wide shallow steps, was considered to be rather less grand than Fortts. The Red House was probably the most popular baker selling a very wide selection of breads, all white of course, we didn't go in for wholemeal or brown in those days except for something called Hovis, which was brown and had the name embossed on the side of every loaf as today. So suspicious of brown were we that when I went to boarding school I had a doctor's certificate to say that I could only eat white bread, the school considering itself very progressive by only using brown bread. Perfectly untrue of course but I was very popular when exchanging my white bread for brown in return for some special favour or other!

The shop window on the left hand side of the entrance was filled with iced cakes, not just the usual round ones but cakes made in all sorts of different shapes, there was one like a mushroom upside-down, coffee probably but the one I remember best looked like a big yellow melon iced on the outside and sponge inside. This was Jean's mother's favourite for her rather formal tea parties, Mrs Fanshawe was a perfectionist and I an extremely nervous school girl and I once had a never to be forgotten disaster on one of these occasions.

The tea table was beautifully laid with Rockingham china, white with a wide pale apricot band and a gold decoration of ferns and leaves with a very special deep circular dish on a high stem with a lid for the jam. The jam was always the same an unusual rather runny golden Cape Gooseberry from South Africa which was sold by Caters in tins. Somehow when attempting to pass it I managed to knock the whole thing over and runny sticky jam poured out and spread across the lace table cloth and polished table, what happened next is a complete blank but I am sure that I was not invited to tea again for a very long time.

Lastly I must tell you about 'Evans and Owens' a delightful old fashioned department store as large as Jollys but very different. An imposing building built on the steep slope of Bartlett Street so that the upper storey was entered at street level from Alfred Street opposite the Assembly Rooms, while the main entrance was much further down the hill.

Evans and Owens department store

On the top floor there was a small café and the millinery department, much less glamorous than Jollys and without a Miss Hulbert, with a wide metal spiral staircase down into the main shop.

The main entrance opened on to a wide aisle running the length of the shop with all the various departments leading off it. Like Jollys they sold almost everything except food and there was even a Post Office. This is the only shop which I can remember that still used the exciting system for paying and getting change via a network of little overhead railway tracks linking every department with a central cash desk. An assistant would put the bill and your cash inside a small wooden ball which unscrewed, and send it speeding across the shop to the cashier high up in her cubby hole who would send it clattering back with the change. If there was an odd farthing in the change this would come not as a coin but a small strip of paper with a couple of dozen or so pins 'a farthings worth of pins' was very useful.

The former Evans and Owens building in 2004

A very popular and useful department was the Haberdashery Department where everything was sold separately or by the yard, elastic in different widths and colours, sewing silks and cottons on solid wooden reels, knitting needles, wools and patterns and an absolute rainbow of ribbons. There were vicious looking hat pins with coloured knobs, with hair still done up into 'buns' it was possible to skewer through the back of a hat and make it safe in any wind or weather. The selection of buttons was wonderful, they came in every size and shape right down to tiny pearl ones, and were all stitched on to display cards, the assistant would cut off however many you needed even if it was only one or two. Although every household had its button box, nothing was discarded until the buttons had been cut off, new buttons were always needed for the dressmakers.

At the far end of the main aisle discreetly shielded from public view was the department which sold ladies and children's underwear, this was where we came to buy our Chilprufe vests and combinations, strange garments but beautifully warm, as well as that indispensable garment called a 'Liberty bodice', these were a sort of padded cotton waist coat worn over the vest or 'combies', which came down over the hips and for the older girls had suspenders attached for our stockings. We also needed warm woollen knickers also made by Chilprufe, usually in navy blue with elastic at the waist and legs

My mother's generation still wore corsets, she continued to wear hers all her life right up into the 1980s. In pale pink or white they were like an armour all whalebone, hooks and eyes and laces from top to bottom, Evans and Owens had a corset maker, but it was more usual for the 'Spirella' lady to come to the house to measure and fit a corset individually, the Spirella lady's visits were quite an event!

High up on Evans and Owen's roof were two large metal letters E and O, they were painted black and were perforated by little holes, to let the wind through I suppose, because the shop was high up these could be seen from a distance. I got to know those two letters very well because our dentist's surgery which was in one of the houses on the high pavement at the top of Milsom Street, was at the back and faced out towards them, and as I sat in the chair I could see them above a tank

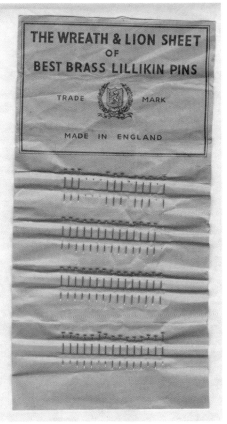

A sheet of pins, as sold by Evans and Owens

of gold fish which he had in the window. I visited the dentist a good many times to be fitted with various plates and gold bands to straighten my rather protruding front teeth, successfully I am glad to say! He also had a fascinating gadget in his waiting room, called I think, an 'Epidiascope' into which you slotted a postcard at one end and viewed it through two eye pieces which magically gave a 3D effect although I am sure there was more to it than that.

One thing which was very different from today, all your purchases, apart from food which went into paper bags, were carefully wrapped in good strong paper, usually brown, although Jollys was green, and tied with string. If it was a convenient size you would carry it home in a shopping basket, otherwise every shop had a delivery service and often your parcel would get home before you did. The bigger shops like Jollys had a van, but most had an 'errand boy'. Errand boys had tricycles with very large square baskets over the front wheel, or in some cases a large box like container with a lid and the shops name, better for wet weather. For some reason the errand boys were renowned for their whistling, and very tuneful they were whistling their way round the town to the latest catchy music hall tunes.

Christmas

W ITH ALL FOUR OF MY GRANDPARENTS living within walking distance of each other we had a double celebration on Christmas day, on alternate years we would have lunch at 'Number Five' and tea at Richmond House or a visit to 'Number Five' and dinner in the evening at Richmond House.

The idea of any shop being open on Christmas day was unthinkable although there was always a delivery of letters and cards on Christmas morning. Evidently the poor postman was different although this was when he was given his 'Christmas Box', a thank you in cash from most of the houses on his round and probably a mince pie and sherry or something in the kitchens as he went, so perhaps it was not too bad.

The two celebrations were very different, at 'Number Five' all was still delightfully traditional while at Richmond House things were more lavish, both were cheerful happy occasions and lots of fun.

At 'Number Five' there was always an enormous goose brought over from Grannie's home in County Cork in Ireland by one or other of her sisters. The lunch was late, never before half past two and if ever a table could be said to groan with food this one did. There was that enormous goose delicious with its dark rich meat and crispy skin, vast quantities of vegetables and apple sauce, all followed by an equally large dark rich Christmas pudding carried in to noisy cheers blazing with flaming brandy.

Inside the pudding were treasures to be found, a silver thimble which meant that the finder would be 'an old maid', or a silver ring, for marriage, as well as silver coins. Real silver in those days, shillings, sixpences and even a few tiny three penny bits, the ring and the thimble were handed back ready for next year but we could keep the coins. While I am mentioning money real gold guineas (one pound, one shilling) and half guineas were still legal currency and in everyday use, Grandpa Owen always gave us a gold guinea for Christmas and birthdays and a gold half guinea was the usual 'tip' before going back to school, of course we spent them how I wish that I had saved one or two!

Although the house was decorated with holly and ivy there was no Christmas tree, instead Grannie and Grandpa handed out the presents from a decorated table, the presents were much simpler and less expensive than today's, but I think that they probably gave as much or even more pleasure. At 'Number Five' there was always one present we could be sure to receive and that was a new wooden hoop, a size larger each year. Hoops were popular toys sold from bunches hanging outside shops.

After lunch while the grown ups relaxed we would be sent out to join the other children bowling their new hoops on the broad sweep of the Crescent pavement before setting off to walk over Zion Hill and on down Primrose Hill to Richmond House. Hoops are certainly not dull toys they require considerable practise and skill with the sticks to control and guide them, and with imagination they can become everything from a circus horse to a train, and until well after the second world war one of a Brownie's tests was to be able to bowl a hoop in a figure of eight.

At Richmond House Grannie Owen did not believe in stinting at Christmas, the house was decorated from top to toe and in the hall would be a tall Christmas tree lit by dozens of little wax candles in small metal holders which clipped on to the ends of the branches. I still have a few of those candle clips, they were so much prettier than any string of electric lights and surprisingly seldom caught fire, I cannot remember it ever happening although there was always a bucket of water hidden nearby.

For our dinner in the evening we put on our party dresses and the grown ups wore evening dress. Every year the table would be decorated with greenery and crackers and in the centre of it all was a wonderful pyramid made with delicious crystallised fruits, (from Caters I expect!).

At Richmond House we had a turkey instead of a goose, goose had always been the traditional bird for Christmas and turkey was something new, otherwise everything followed more or less the same pattern as at 'Number Five'.

Then came Boxing Day and our annual visit to the pantomime at the Theatre Royal. This was Grandfather Owen's big day, he would take several adjoining 'boxes' at the back of the Dress Circle and fill them with aunts, uncles, cousins and children of all ages and sizes.

Dressed in party clothes with our programmes and boxes of chocolates we all entered into the spirit of a good old fashioned slapstick pantomime, singing the latest popular songs, booing the villain and cheering the hero, it was the happiest of afternoons. At the end we trooped across the road and up the little narrow cobbled streets to Milsom Street and tea at Fortts.

Here friendly waiters had pushed together several tables and kept us supplied with plates of hot buttered toast, tiny sandwiches and as many Bath buns and cream cakes, and of course Chocolate Olivers as we could eat, dear Grandpa I am sure that he got as much pleasure from that annual treat as we did.

Growing Up

W ITH THE DEPARTURE to boarding school we began to grow up and move away from the childhood which I have tried to recall and describe.

In spite of the trauma of my arrival at boarding school I soon settled and the years passed happily as I made my way up through the hierarchy of school life to become first a prefect and eventually head girl. It was a fitting end to all those years at school and I travelled back to Bath by train to be met by a jubilant Jean, we were ready for whatever challenges lay ahead.

I have tried to give you an idea of what it was like to grow up in Bath in the early 20th century, there is of course much still to be told but this must suffice for the time being.

I hope that this little book has amused and shown you that although Bath has a reputation world wide for its architecture and Roman Baths and as a place for retirement and healing, it is also a vibrant and happy place in which to grow up.

Angie and Jean, the two friends who grow up in this book

What Happened Later
A Short Appendix

Ruth trained as a physiotherapist and in 1939 joined the Army medical service and went to India where she remained 'till the end of the war. She married John Byrne an Army doctor and they returned to live in Bath with their three sons. She died in 2003.

Honor married just before the war. She joined the FANYS (Field Ambulance nursing Yeomanry) in 1939 and with her flying experience was one of those given the task of flying planes from the factories to their operational bases. This led to her death in 1941 when the Wellington bomber she was flying crashed into a hillside in thick fog.

Jean trained as a nurse at the Middlesex Hospital in London and in 1940 joined the Army nursing service as a 'QA' Queen Alexandra's nurse. She too went to India and remained there until the end of the war. She married Norman McQueen an Army doctor, they returned to live in Edinburgh with their four children.

Angie joined the Red Cross V.A.D (Voluntary Aid Detachment) and became Commandant of the Wiltshire 36 Detachment (Warminster). She trained as a Home Office lecturer in Chemical Warfare and Air Raid Precautions. In 1938 she married John Willoughby an Army Officer and remained in Wiltshire throughout the war producing three children in 1940, 1942 and 1946.

Jean and Angie remain the friends that they have been for almost their entire lives, well over 80 years!